SUPERHUMAN SCIENCE

SUPERHUMAN HEARING

Jessica Rusick

Big Buddy Books

An Imprint of Abdo Publishing
abdobooks.com

abdobooks.com

Published by Abdo Publishing, a division of ABDO, PO Box 398166, Minneapolis, Minnesota 55439. Copyright © 2022 by Abdo Consulting Group, Inc. International copyrights reserved in all countries. No part of this book may be reproduced in any form without written permission from the publisher. Big Buddy Books™ is a trademark and logo of Abdo Publishing.

Printed in the United States of America, North Mankato, Minnesota
102021
012022

Design: Emily O'Malley, Mighty Media, Inc.
Production: Mighty Media, Inc.
Editor: Rebecca Felix
Cover Photographs: Shutterstock Images
Interior Photographs: © Harald Krichel/CC BY-SA 3.0/Wikimedia Commons, p. 19; PopTech/Flickr, p. 15; Shutterstock Images, pp. 5, 7, 9, 11, 13, 17, 21, 25, 27, 29; TEDxUNC/Flickr, p. 23
Design Elements: Shutterstock Images

Library of Congress Control Number: 2021942810

Publisher's Cataloging-in-Publication Data
Names: Rusick, Jessica, author.
Title: Superhuman hearing / by Jessica Rusick
Description: Minneapolis, Minnesota : Abdo Publishing, 2022 | Series: Superhuman science | Includes online resources and index.
Identifiers: ISBN 9781532197017 (lib. bdg.) | ISBN 9781644947173 (pbk.) | ISBN 9781098219147 (ebook)
Subjects: LCSH: Human physiology--Juvenile literature. | Performance--Juvenile literature. | Ability--Juvenile literature. | Hearing--Juvenile literature. | Super powers--Juvenile literature.
Classification: DDC 599.9--dc23

DON'T TRY THIS AT HOME

Many of the superhuman feats described in this series were overseen by trainers and doctors. Do not attempt to re-create these feats. Doing so could cause injury.

CONTENTS

Amazing Ability 4

What Is Hearing? 6

How Humans Hear 8

Volume & Pitch 10

Echolocation 12

Musical Marvel 16

Synesthesia 20

Tensor Tympani 24

Echo Power 28

Glossary 30

Online Resources 31

Index 32

AMAZING ABILITY

Superheroes have superpowers. But real men and women also have **incredible** abilities. Some people hear **amazingly** well. They have superhuman hearing!

People who can hear small distinctions in music are sometimes called Golden Ears.

WHAT IS HEARING?

Hearing is the process of **perceiving** sound. Sound is made of **vibrations**. These vibrations travel in sound waves. The waves go through the air and into our ears.

Vibrations are how guitars produce sound. A plucked string vibrates. Its sound is made louder by the guitar's hollow body.

HOW HUMANS HEAR

Our ears have three parts. The outer ear collects sound waves, or **vibrations**. The middle ear makes the vibrations louder. The inner ear turns the vibrations into electrical **signals**. These signals travel to your brain. Your brain recognizes the signals as sounds.

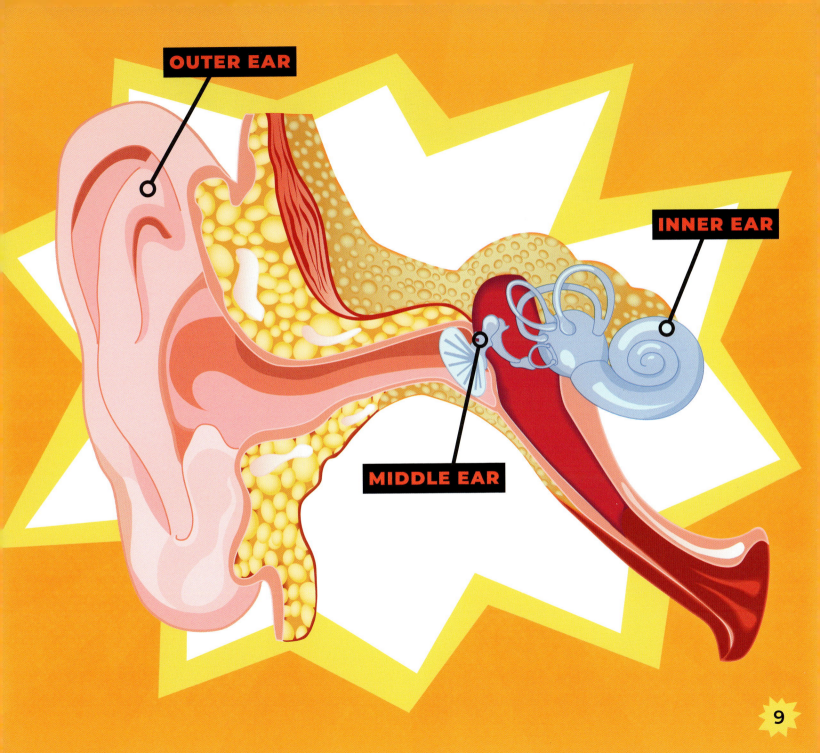

VOLUME & PITCH

A sound's volume is how loud or soft it is. A sound's pitch is how high or low it is. Objects that **vibrate** slowly make low-pitched sounds. Objects that vibrate quickly make high-pitched sounds. Humans can only hear sounds within a certain range of pitches.

Dogs can hear much higher pitches than humans can.

ECHOLOCATION

Echoes happen when sound waves bounce off objects. The waves bounce back and create a copy of the original sound. Some animals use echoes to locate objects! This is called **echolocation**.

BOUNCING SOUND

Sound waves bounce best off hard surfaces. Soft surfaces absorb sound waves.

Dolphins use echolocation to navigate, find prey, and avoid predators.

Daniel Kish is blind. He uses **echolocation** to help **navigate**. Kish clicks his tongue. Then, he listens for **echoes** that bounce off nearby objects. Kish learns information about where he is based on how the echoes sound. He can tell an object's size, location, and more by listening closely!

Daniel Kish has taught hundreds of people how to echolocate.

MUSICAL MARVEL

In music, pitches are named as music notes. There are seven main notes. Musicians are often **sensitive** to pitch. Many can hear small differences between music notes.

In an orchestra, different instruments create different pitches and sounds. These blend together to create beautiful music!

Jacob Collier is a musician. He has a **rare** ability called absolute pitch. Collier can correctly name the music note of any pitch he hears. He can also **identify** and sing microtones. These are pitches in between standard music notes. Collier's abilities allow him to create songs with **complex** harmonies.

RARE SKILL

Scientists believe only one in every 10,000 people has absolute pitch.

Jacob Collier has performed his music at concerts all over the world.

SYNESTHESIA

Have you ever heard a color or tasted a sound? People with synesthesia may have! Humans have five senses. Each sense is tied to a part of the brain. People with synesthesia have connections between these different parts. This allows some of their senses to blend together.

Synesthesia affects people differently. For example, a particular sound might sound blue to one person and green to another.

Melissa McCracken is an artist. She has chromesthesia. This form of synesthesia lets her see colors when she hears sounds! McCracken sees colors in her head when she listens to a song. She uses her ability to make art. McCracken listens to a song. Then, she paints the song in color!

FAMOUS EARS

Musicians Lady Gaga, Lorde, and Pharrell Williams have chromesthesia.

In 2018, Melissa McCracken gave a speech about what having synesthesia has taught her.

TENSOR TYMPANI

Loud noises can damage your ears. The tensor tympani muscle helps protect you. When loud noises enter the ear, the muscle contracts. This softens the noises.

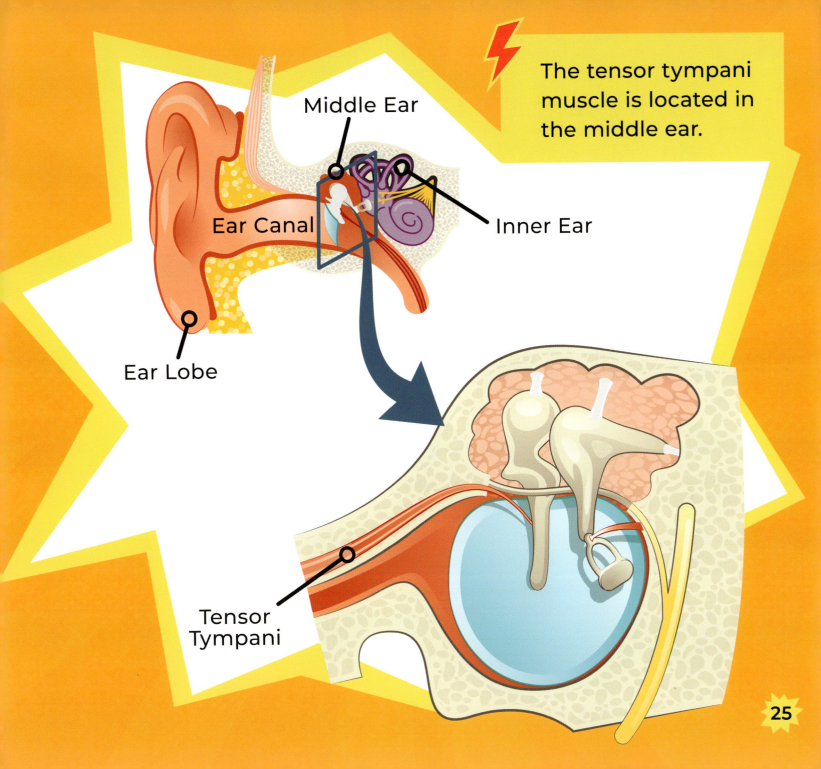

Try yawning. Do you hear rumbling in your ears? That's your tensor tympani muscle! Many people hear it when yawning. Certain people have the **rare** ability to make this muscle rumble on command. Some people with this skill use it to drown out unwanted noise.

Some people who can tense their tensor tympani muscle on command squeeze their eyes shut tightly to perform this feat.

27

ECHO POWER

Want to improve your hearing skills? Practice **echolocation**!

1. Close your eyes.
2. Have someone hold a large, hard object near you.
3. Click your tongue against the roof of your mouth. Keep clicking and turn your head from side to side.

4. Listen carefully as you continue to click and turn your head. Can you tell where the object is?

GLOSSARY

amazingly—in a way that causes wonder or surprise.

complex—having many parts, details, ideas, or functions.

echo (EH-koh)—a repeated sound caused by a sound hitting something and bouncing back.

echolocation (eh-koh-loh-KAY-shuhn)—a process for locating distant or unseen objects by using sound waves.

identify—to find out what something is.

incredible—amazing or unbelievable.

navigate—to find the way from place to place.

perceive (puhr-SEEV)—to use the senses to become aware of something.

rare—uncommon or not often found or seen.

sensitive—able to quickly and easily feel or notice.

signal—something that gives warning or a command.

vibrate (VEYE-brayt)—to move back and forth very fast. This movement is called a vibration.

ONLINE RESOURCES

To learn more about superhuman hearing, please visit **abdobooklinks.com** or scan this QR code. These links are routinely monitored and updated to provide the most current information available.

INDEX

absolute pitch, 18
animals, 11, 12, 13
art, 22

brain, 8, 20

chromesthesia, 22
Collier, Jacob, 18, 19
colors, 20, 21, 22

echoes, 12, 14
echolocation, 12, 13, 14, 15, 28, 29
echolocation activity, 28, 29
electrical signals, 8

inner ear, 8, 9, 25

Kish, Daniel, 14, 15

Lady Gaga, 22
Lorde, 22

McCracken, Melissa, 22, 23
microtones, 18
middle ear, 8, 9, 25
music, 5, 16, 17, 18, 19, 22

outer ear, 8, 9

pitch, 10, 11, 16, 17, 18

sound waves, 6, 8, 12
superheroes, 4
synesthesia, 20, 21, 22, 23

taste, 20
tensor tympani, 24, 25, 26, 27

vibrations, 6, 7, 8, 10
volume, 10

Williams, Pharrell, 22

yawning, 26